ENDORSEMENTS

People's Opening, Liverpool Capital of Culture ©Liverpool City Council

I remember being delighted when I read the first ISAN guide – a practical, pragmatic, down to earth safety guide for street events. Too many potentially exciting worthwhile events are being cancelled. Why? A complete and utter lack of understanding and a serious risk aversion. This new guide could be entitled Taking Creativity Seriously. It clearly demonstrates what needs to be done, particularly in relation to risk management and risk assessments. This to-the-point guide is factual, clear, concise and extremely helpful. Its use should help facilitate new, diverse, exciting events whilst ensuring people's safety, and compliance with the law.

I commend it to all those involved in these types of events.

Richard Limb, Director of Leisure Safety, Capita Symonds
President of National Outdoor Event Association
CFIOSH,FRSPH,CMIEH,DMS

The Licensing Act 2003 has changed the way in which Street Arts events are organised and managed, placing more onus on the individual operator. The Institute of Licensing is pleased to support ISAN's Safety Guidance, which offers clear and practical guidance to those who wish to provide arts events outside of the confines of licensed buildings such as pubs, theatres or cinemas. The guidance complements the advice in the HSE's Event Safety Guide, the expertise of local authority licensing officers and local Safety Advisory Groups, (where established). The Institute recommends this updated guide is used by all event organisers, local authorities and Institute members as a helpful source of information and advice.

Jeffrey Leib, The Institute of Licensing

FOREWORD

Beautiful People, Tavaziva Dance Company, SIRF. Gilmar Ribeiro. gilmarribeiro.com

This guidance has been produced by the Independent Street Arts Network (ISAN). ISAN is a membership-led professional organisation for producers, presenters, artists and support agencies that promote Street Arts. ISAN exists to support its members and the general development of the Street Arts sector in the UK through networking, information sharing, collaboration, lobbying, training and advocacy.

This edition of Safety Guidance for Street Arts, Carnival, Processions and Large Scale Events has been comprehensively updated to cover the Licensing Act 2003 (England and Wales), and current legislation in Scotland and Nothern Ireland.

ISAN recognised in 2002 that no specific safety guidance for this sector existed and that other publications such as the Event Safety Guide made only passing reference to Street Arts. To fill this gap ISAN commissioned David Bilton, then of Event International Ltd, to compile appropriate guidance.

The first edition, published in 2004 was the result of wide consultation within the sector over the proceeding two years. Special thanks go to David Bilton for the resulting document, which has proved to be ISAN's most popular publication. Thanks also to Bill Gee and Jeremy Shine, and the many other members of ISAN who alongside experts from local authority licensing, building inspectorate and emergency planning departments, police, event and security companies took the time and trouble to read and comment on various drafts

This guidance has now been updated in line with current licensing legislation and its effects on Street Arts events. In producing this thoroughly revised and freshly illustrated edition ISAN is particularly grateful for comments and input from Jeffrey Leib, Institute of Licensing, and Richard Limb, President of the National Outdoor Event Association and from ISAN board members.

It is imperative that any information provided in this document is applied appropriately to the local context of the event in question. Advice and clarification must be sought from local licensing, health and safety, emergency service and other sources. It is intended that the information contained here may assist in informing these agencies of the specific considerations when planning Street Arts events and thus should be shared with them.

We hope that we have demystified and debunked the issues that can prove a barrier to organising successful outdoor arts events.

Julian Rudd – ISAN Co-ordinator
Christine Hathway – ISAN Project Manager

Disclaimer: as guidance ISAN can accept no responsibility or liability for the application of the information herein contained to specific individual circumstances. This responsibility and liability must continue to lie with the specific event organiser in their local circumstance.

CONTENTS

01 INTRODUCTION

Picnic, Dancing City. G+DIF 2007, Briony Campbell

This Safety Guidance is designed to consider the provisions that need to be made to ensure that Street Arts, Carnival, Processions and Large-scale Performances can be enjoyed by the general public and performers in a safe environment. These activities take place in public places, are often free of charge, and have a broad appeal to a wide age range with a particular emphasis on families; as such they require different considerations to more formal entertainment. It is unlikely that a child or dog from the audience will walk on stage during a performance of Shakespeare – this is very likely during a Street Arts performance!

02 DEFINITIONS

A Midsummer Night's Tree, SIRF ©Gilmar Ribeiro, gilmarribeiro.com

2.1 STREET ARTS

Street Arts is the umbrella term, used in the UK, given to performances in various genres (theatre, dance, circus, spectacle, music or any combination of the above) that are created for outdoor public spaces – sometimes in the street, or in town squares, parks and other public spaces. Street Arts has a purposefully wide definition and is inclusive of solo performances through to large scale spectacle and from community processional projects to stunning outdoor interactive visual installations. In other European countries, in particular in France and Spain, Street Arts is seen as an important art form in its own right, attracting sustained investment from local and national government. The French term, "theatre without walls" is a useful definition.

Street Arts events are socially and culturally inclusive. In an international context, British Street Arts companies are leading the way in creating work that reflects the cultural diversity of a nation.

Street Arts is a uniquely democratic forum in which to work, since public spaces 'belong' to everyone and art that is designed to be performed in such a space is owned and accessible to us all. In the UK Street Arts engage with audiences counted in their millions every year. These large and diverse audiences enjoy performances and events together without the barriers sometimes found in traditional arts venues. This exciting dynamic is perhaps what attracts so many of us to the Street Arts environment – it is an antidote to our increasing national obsession with the cult of celebrity, of TV, video games and the internet. Street Arts is always live, always in public space, always with an atmosphere of unpredictability.

The types of performance can be further defined as "static", or "walkabout".

2.1.1 STATIC PERFORMANCES are performances where most of the performance takes place within a clearly defined area; this could be as formal as a stage or as informal as a rope laid out on the ground. The audience stands or sits to watch this performance.

2.1.2 WALKABOUT PERFORMANCES are shows where the performer moves and interacts either verbally or physically with passers by. Examples of this type of performance are a stilt walker in costume who may talk to the public; a street band who follow individuals down the street, or a character in costume.

Malaya, Close Act, SIRF ©Gilmar Ribeiro, gilmarribeiro.com

2.2 CARNIVALS AND PROCESSIONS are performances that take place along a linear route with a designated start and finish point (although this may be a circular route starting and finishing in the same place). These may include vehicles (motorised and non-motorised) and elaborately costumed performers on foot.

2.3 LARGE-SCALE PERFORMANCES are shows that may be either "static" or "processions" or include elements of both. An example of a static large-scale performance may be an outdoor theatre performance featuring lights, music, water, pyrotechnics, or aerial trapeze. A procession may involve parading large vehicles, inflatables or structures through the streets. At night they often involve pyrotechnics; there is separate guidance available for specific firework only displays (see following page).

03 SCOPE OF THIS GUIDE

3.1 This guidance is not exhaustive but is designed to assist you to develop a safe plan for your event. Each event of this type will have its own unique circumstances created either by the performance or the location and your plan must take account of these peculiarities. Legally it should be noted that, as with any other work activity, all events are covered by The Health & Safety at Work etc. Act 1974.

3.2 This guide should be read in conjunction with other key safety publications:

3.2.1 THE EVENT SAFETY GUIDE: A GUIDE TO HEALTH, SAFETY AND WELFARE AT MUSIC AND SIMILAR EVENTS (THE PURPLE BOOK)
(HSE 1999) ISBN 9780717624539

MANAGING CROWDS SAFELY
(HSE 2000) ISBN: 9780717618347

FIVE STEPS TO RISK ASSESSMENT
(HSE) ISBN 0 7176 6189 X

WORKING TOGETHER ON FIREWORK DISPLAYS
(HSE 2006) ISBN: 9780717661961

GUIDE TO SAFETY AT SPORTS GROUNDS (THE GREEN GUIDE)
(The Stationery Office) ISBN: 9780117020740

In addition Local Authorities and Police may have their own safe events policies to which you will have to refer

HSE publications from: www.hse.gov.uk
Stationery Office publication from: www.tsoshop.co.uk

La Machine Image supplied by Northwest Regional Development Agency Photo: Nic Gaunt

04 EVENT ORGANISATION

4·1 RISK ASSESSMENT

Risk assessment is the key aspect of creating a safe environment for any event. "An assessment of risk is nothing more than a careful examination of what could cause harm to people so that you can weigh up whether you have taken enough precautions or should do more". (Health and Safety Executive: Five Steps to Risk Assessment). Risk assessment should be used as a tool to create a safe event and should not be regarded as a "something-which-has-to-be-done-under-sufferance"!

A Risk Assessment approach is essential (as well as a legal requirement when more than 5 employees are involved). A risk assessment should be used to assist not hinder the event management process. It is recommended that this risk assessment is carried out by a competent person and recorded.

Although it is often thought to be a difficult concept to grasp, it is actually a very simple process:

STEP ONE Identify the hazard (anything which has the potential to cause harm to people) – What is the hazard, where is the hazard located?

STEP TWO Identify those people who may be harmed and how

STEP THREE Identify existing precautions e.g. venue design, operational procedures

STEP FOUR Evaluate the risk or likelihood of the hazard affecting people

STEP FIVE Determine the additional measures that need to be imposed to minimise the risk and the likelihood of injury

At this point the risk should be reassessed and if now deemed acceptable, the activity should be allowed to progress. If the risk of an activity cannot be managed to a suitable level then the activity will need to be changed and the process must be repeated from step one.

It is often considered that a Risk Assessment will simply add to the cost by imposing expensive control measures. However this is not necessarily the case – a Risk Assessment will help to create **appropriate** control measures and can actually save money. It is also much easier to develop new, diverse and unorthodox performances if the risks have been properly assessed.

There are a number of formats for creating a risk assessment;

examples are provided at appendix 1. Each event and performance space is unique with its own hazards and organisers should not simply 'cut and paste' from another event risk assessment – whilst some risks are generic each event should be considered as a unique activity.

The remainder of this book will help you to analyse the hazards, risks and control measures necessary for the risk assessment. In addition it is important that the risk assessment is communicated effectively not just to the statutory authorities but also to the team who are creating and managing the performance.

4·2 ASSEMBLING A TEAM

A team of people will be required to manage the event. It is easier for all the interested parties if there is a clear management structure and a person who is designated as the Event Manager who has overall responsibility for the event. This may be the Artistic Director, Production Manager, or Safety Officer depending on the scale of the event – however it is important that this is a senior person within the organisation with the ability to make and implement decisions.

In addition to the Event Manager a number of other roles need to be identified and allocated to individuals. For a small event one person may undertake several roles, but it is still important to be clear about which roles any individual is taking responsibility for.

OUTLINE ROLES AND DUTIES ARE AS FOLLOWS:

4.2.1 ARTISTIC DIRECTOR The person responsible for creating the content of the event. Duties will include sourcing and contracting artists, determining venues and scheduling performances.

4.2.2 SAFETY MANAGER/CO-ORDINATOR Responsible for co-ordinating the overall safety of the public, contractors and sub-contractors and undertaking a risk assessment of the event.

4.2.3 PRODUCTION MANAGER/ASSISTANT PRODUCTION MANAGERS The person(s) responsible for ensuring that the control measures contained within the risk assessment are implemented and that the site infrastructure is specified and installed correctly. They are also responsible for ensuring that all the technical requirements for artists are identified and implemented.

4.2.4 STAGE MANAGERS/ASSISTANT STAGE MANAGERS Responsible for health and safety at the performance area and ensuring events take place on time.

Fanfare, G+DIF 2007. Alastair Muir

4.2.5 TECHNICAL STAFF & CREW All of the stage, sound, light, power and other technicians necessary for creating the event.

4.2.6 AMBULANCE/FIRST AID Usually this is contracted staff from the Local Ambulance trust, private ambulance or the voluntary aid societies e.g. St John Ambulance, Red Cross. There is usually a charge made for these services even by the voluntary societies – ensure there is an agreed level of service and an agreed price prior to the event. The Event Safety Guide has a useful matrix to suggest the number and type of personnel required; however this matrix should only be used as a basis for discussion with first aid services.

4.2.7 STEWARDS Stewards may be volunteers or employed through a professional company. Whether voluntary or professional it is essential that they are clearly identifiable to the public and that at night a high visibility jacket or armband is worn. All stewards should undergo some training to ensure they watch the crowd (not the performance), and receive a thorough briefing on their role at the event. The briefing may be verbal or written (preferably both) and should include as a minimum key details such as emergency evacuation procedures; lost children procedures; location of fire fighting equipment, first aid and communications facilities; names and locations of key personnel. Stewards also need to have the capacity to spot potential troublemakers and quietly intercept them before they reach the performer. Anyone performing a security role in

a paid capacity (other than when directly employed in-house) must be licensed by the Security Industry Authority (see *Security At Events: Guidance on the Private Security Industry Act 2001 – SIA, 2008*).

4.2.8 LOST CHILDREN PERSONNEL Adequate procedures need to be in place for lost children. This should include how to deal with a child who presents themselves as lost and also for parents/guardians who report their child as lost. If an independent Lost Children Point is created it is essential that anyone involved in this process has been vetted by the police through a Criminal Records Bureau (CRB) check to ensure that they are suitable to undertake this role. This check is undertaken by the employer or directly through the CRB by a body that is registered with them to conduct checks. It is illegal to request a check unless the individual is working in a regulated position or who is regularly working, caring for or supervising children.

However within a Street Arts context there will be standard procedures in place for dealing with lost children by the police, shopping centre, or park and the event procedures should dovetail with these provisions.

4.2.9 COMMUNICATION After assembling the team it is important to consider how information is disseminated to the team both before the event and during the event. Prior to the event adequate briefings for all personnel are essential; during the event key people should be in contact by two-way radio and mobile phone.

Flogging a Dead Horse, Paka – Paradise Gardens Festival 2008. Hayley Madden

4.2.10 WELFARE It is also important to consider the welfare of all staff, this is often overlooked in the heat of an event. Adequate facilities and rotas need to be created to ensure that staff are able to fulfill their roles effectively.

4.3 CONSULTATION

4.3.1 At a very early stage the event organiser should consult with a wide variety of people to ensure that the event is feasible. The consultees should include:

→ The landowner or manager of the space
→ The Local Authority
→ Licensing Department
→ Highways Department
→ Health & Safety Department
→ Building Control Department
→ Events Department
→ The emergency services (police, fire and ambulance)

Other people may need to be consulted depending on the circumstances; for example the local Residents Association should be consulted for an event in the middle of a housing estate. Be sensitive when planning the location and timing of events; for example noise may interfere with religious services (and vice-versa) and other users of the venue such as street traders should be considered.

Many Local Authorities have created a formal Safety Advisory Group (SAG) or Multi-Agency Group (MAG) where all of these organisations are brought together which makes consultation easier. The Chair of this group is usually located within the Local Authority but may be in any one of a number of departments e.g. Building Control, Health & Safety, Licensing, or Leisure.

4.3.2 BRIEFING DOCUMENT The timing of the initial consultation should be carefully considered – particularly for new events. Preparing a briefing document which gives an outline of the event at an early stage is a useful way to enable key personnel to engage with the event and they often welcome the opportunity to assist with the event management process. This outline should include:

→ Dates and times
→ Venue
→ Brief description of the event
→ Anticipated audience size and profile
→ Outline management arrangements

It should be noted that people hate being asked to make decisions at a late stage particularly with inadequate information; this reluctance has been exacerbated by the Dreamscape tragedy at Chester-le-Street. However it can also be counter-productive to try to consult without sufficient information – so the timing needs to be carefully considered.

4.3.3 EVENT MANUAL From this initial briefing document and the responses to it an Event Manual can be created. This should be a working document that can be updated and circulated until the event. There are various forms of Event Manuals and some Local authorities have a standard Event Manual form – check Local Authority websites for details. This document should contain as a minimum:

→ Event details
→ Dates/times
→ Venue(including venue assessment)
→ Anticipated audience (numbers and composition)
→ Site plan
→ Organisation and Management structure (including communications)
→ Stewarding (including crowd management)
→ Medical arrangements
→ Traffic Management
→ Welfare (including sanitary arrangements)
→ Emergency procedures (including cancellation planning)
→ Risk Assessment

It is important that the contents of the Event Manual are agreed by all the relevant parties and often there will be a meeting close to the event where this Event Manual will be 'signed off' or there may be an 'electronic' sign off of the event manual.

4.3.4 CANCELLATION PLANNING In a worst-case scenario an event or part of an event may need to be cancelled. A clear procedure for canceling an event or part of event should be part of the planning process. In all instances it should be clear who has the responsibility to stop the event and this may be different depending on the circumstances. E.g. If a fault is spotted with regard to event equipment which could cause injury the Stage Manager or Production Manager should be given the authority to stop the show; if there is a report of high winds later in the day this will require input from the artists, the Police and Local Authority to inform the decision of the Event Organiser. Communicating decisions to the public through on site PA announcements/signage and off site web/local radio announcements is also a vital part of the process.

4.3.5 DEBRIEF After the event a full debrief should be held with all parties to evaluate the event and make recommendations for future years.

4.4 LICENSING AND PERFORMING RIGHTS SOCIETY

Licenses for outdoor events are governed by a variety of legislation depending on which of the four UK nations the event is taking place in; in addition reference needs to be made to local byelaws. The most appropriate way to proceed is to consult the relevant Local Authority Licensing Department for further information; a brief synopsis of each country's legislation is outlined below.

4.4.1 ENGLAND & WALES Events are now licensed under the 2003 Licensing Act. This replaced the previous Public Entertainments Licence and also brought the responsibility for licensing alcohol under the control of the Local Authority rather than the Magistrates Court as was the previous arrangement. The stated aims of the Act are:

1 the prevention of crime and disorder;
2 public safety;
3 the prevention of public nuisance; and
4 the protection of children from harm.

Licences are required if the event contains 'licensable activities':

→ The sale by retail of alcohol
→ The provision of regulated entertainment, and
→ The provision of late night refreshment

Regulated entertainment is generally taken to include any of the following:

a the performance of a play
b an exhibition of film(s)
c an indoor sporting event
d a boxing or wrestling entertainment
e a performance of live music
f any playing of recorded music
g a performance of dance, and
h entertainment of a similar description to (e), (f) or (g) above.

Regulated entertainment may also include the provision of facilities for making music or dancing or entertainment of a similar description.

EXEMPTIONS The Licensing Act 2003 makes the following exemptions (relevant to this Guide) to the definition of regulated entertainment:-

Entertainment and associated facilities provided at a garden fete or other function / event of similar character is NOT a regulated entertainment (unless promoted with a view to applying any part of its proceeds for purposes of private gain).

The performance of morris dancing, dancing of similar nature or a performance of unamplified, live music which is an integral part of such a performance and associated facilities is NOT a regulated entertainment. Entertainment and associated facilities provided on vehicles in motion is NOT a regulated entertainment.

LATE NIGHT REFRESHMENT Late night refreshment is defined as the provision or supply of hot food or drink between the hours of 23:00pm and 05:00am to any member of the public, on or from any premises, whether for consumption on or off the premises. A licence is not therefore needed for activities such as stand-up comedy, circus performances, fire-eating or incidental/background music. In cases of doubt, contact the local authority licensing team for advice,

All outdoor events are likely to require a licence – even if no alcohol is being served. It is an offence to carry on, or attempt to carry on a licensable activity without, or not in accordance with the relevant authorisation. The sentence on conviction of this offence is a fine of up to £20,000, or up to six months' imprisonment, or both. (www.culture.gov.uk)

There are two means of obtaining a licence:

TEMPORARY EVENT NOTICE (TEN) This is by far the simplest way of obtaining a licence but it does have restrictions:

→ the number of times a person (the "premises user") may apply for a temporary event notice (50 times per year for a personal licence holder and 5 times per year for other people);
→ the number of times a temporary event notice may be given in respect of any particular premises (12 times in a calendar year);
→ the length of time a temporary event may last is (96 hours, although another TEN can be obtained for the same premises providing there has been a 24 hour break);
→ the maximum aggregate duration of the periods covered by temporary event notices at any individual premises (15 days); and
→ the scale of the event in terms of the maximum number of people attending at any one time (less than 500).

The cost of this licence is relatively small and application is usually by a simple form obtained from the Local Authority licensing department (usually on their website or from www.culture.gov.uk). Only the police can object to this application on the grounds of crime and disorder within 48 hours of receipt. The form must be submitted to the local council with the relevant fee and to the police no less than 10 clear working days before the event is due to start – weekends and Bank Holidays are not included in this calculation.

If the police raise objections, organisers will usually be able to negotiate with them to satisfy their concerns. If they persist, the notice will be referred to a committee of councilors to decide whether the event can take place.

PREMISES LICENCE Many Local Authorities have now taken the decision to licence their main outdoor event spaces such as parks, town centres and open spaces where events are regularly held. The Department of Culture, Media & Sport holds a Register of Licensed Public Space in England and Wales (www.culture.gov.uk). If the space is licensed the event will need to be discussed with the holder of the Premises Licence as each space will have different stipulations. However providing that the event falls within the parameters of the licensable activities this should be a relatively straightforward process and the Licensee will determine if the event can take place.

If the area is not licensed an application will need to be submitted for the space. This application will need to be available for public consultation for 28 days and is inevitably a more complex process so sufficient time needs to be allowed – at least 2 to 3 months should be built into the planning timeframe of the event to obtain a licence.

The cost of this licence is set down by the Government, but for large events over 5,000 it is variable depending on the Authority and the number of people expected at the event; the Licensing Authority will advise further on a case by case basis.

ALCOHOL If it is planned to provide alcohol at the event there is a requirement to have a Designated Premises Supervisor (DPS) named on a premises licence (but not for Temporary Event Notices). This is a nominated contact person for the statutory authorities, and must hold a Personal Licence under the Licensing Act to sell alcohol.

4.4.2 LICENSING (SCOTLAND) Events in Scotland are governed by the Civic Government (Scotland) Act 1982 – Section 41. Outdoor events are not required to be licensed under this legislation providing that it is a free event; any event with an entry fee will require a Public Entertainment licence from the Local Authority.

Processions and parades will need to be discussed with the Local Authority and many of them have separate forms to complete e.g. Edinburgh.

Alcohol is governed by the Licensing (Scotland) Act 2005. Application must be made by an individual to the local licensing board for a licence.

4.4.3 LICENSING (NORTHERN IRELAND) Events in Northern Ireland are governed by the Local Government (Miscellaneous Provisions) (Northern Ireland) Order 1985. Outdoor events providing Public Entertainment do require a licence and these can be obtained through the Local Authority Licencing Department.

Under the terms of the The Licensing (Northern Ireland) Order 1996 a licence to sell alcohol on an occasional basis should be made through the local Magistrates Court.

Under Section 2(1) of the Public Processions (Northern Ireland) Act 1998 application for any processions need to be made to the Parades Commission.

Compost Mentis, Whalley Range All Stars, ESSEXstreetdiversions. Mike Byford

4.4.4 PERFORMING RIGHTS SOCIETY (www.mcps-prs-alliance.co.uk)
By law under the Copyright, Designs and Patents Act 1988, if music
is used in public (i.e. outside of the home), permission of every writer
or composer of the music is required. The Performing Rights Society
simplifies this process; refer to the website for further details on
applying for a licence.

4.4.5 PHONOGRAPHIC PERFORMANCE LIMITED (www.pppluk.com) If
you are broadcasting recorded music to the public you should obtain
a PPL licence. The website provides a good guide to the process for
obtaining a licence.

4.5 RECORDING ACCIDENTS AND INCIDENTS

A clear procedure for recording accidents and incidents should be
created for each event. It may be appropriate to seek advice from
your insurance company to ensure that this procedure will be to their
satisfaction. As well as being important for any investigation that may
need to be undertaken after the event, it is also a valuable
management tool in analysing how future event management can be
improved.

Under the Reporting of Injuries, Diseases and Dangerous
Occurrences Regulations 1995, employers must report any
work-related deaths, injuries, cases of disease, or near misses
involving employees wherever they are working by calling the

HSE Incident Contact Centre as soon as possible on 0845 300 9923
(Monday to Friday, 8.30 am to 5 pm), or report online via
www.hse.gov.uk/riddor/report.htm

Accidents and incidents should be reported to the HSE (or local
enviromental health officer) out of hours in the following
circumstances:

→ fatal accidents at work;

→ accidents where several workers have been seriously injured;

→ accidents resulting in serious injury to a member of the public;

→ accidents and incidents causing major disruption

If you are in control of premises, you must report any work-related
deaths and injuries to members of the public and self-employed
people on your premises, and near miss incidents that occur on your
premises.

Flower Power, Flaming Fun. ESSEXstreetdiversions 2008. Paul Starr

Outdoor events have their own constraining features which are different to indoor events. The following list of questions is not exhaustive but is a useful start to identifying individual venue considerations:

5.1 Is the location large enough and suitable for the performance and its intended audience? What are the access/egress/emergency evacuation routes?

5.2 Are there other activities happening at the same time? Who are the other users of the venue – consider people such as street traders, shopkeepers, and delivery routes. Will the performances conflict with this activity? Do other people need to be consulted/involved in the process? Are there pavement cafes that need to be taken into account, or roads, cycle paths or footways that need to be closed?

5.3 What are the hazards in the location? Examples of hazards could be street furniture suitable for climbing, and water features. Do a site visit looking for the hazards, make a note and implement measures to minimise them. Be careful to include hazards that may be there at the time of the event e.g. future electricity/gas/water works, football matches and temporary features such as Christmas Decorations.

5.4 What day and time is the performance? Performances at night and on busy shopping days will have different considerations to a quiet Sunday afternoon. Performances in areas with vibrant alcohol-led night-time economies will need particularly careful planning.

5.5 What is the bad weather provision? If it rains is there a facility to take some or all of the performances into a covered area? In the event of rain on grass is there straw/sand/trackway close by?

5.6 What are the problems with creating the venue infrastructure? Is there vehicular access? Will the surface cope with the weight loading of a particular structure or vehicle?

5.7 How will information be communicated to the general public? Before the event (marketing and press)? During the event (public address announcements and signage)?

5.8 What impact will the venue's location have on nearby residents and businesses? A performance in a town centre may lead to crowds blocking shop entrances for example, affecting that shop's customers. Performances outside domestic premises may interfere with residents, particularly during the evening or at weekends. Do performances near schools, places of worship or licensed premises have appropriate content?

6.1 AUDIENCE SIZE

6.1.1 As these types of event are often free the number of people in the audience may be difficult to predict. To a certain extent this type of audience is self-regulating in that if people cannot see the performance they will simply move on.

6.1.2 However a maximum capacity for the venue should be determined. According to The Event Safety Guide the absolute maximum number of people can be calculated by determining the available audience area in square metres (excluding space taken up by physical obstructions such as stalls, furniture, stages) and multiplying by two; however if a family audience is expected this figure will have to be reduced to take account of buggies, wheelchairs, children etc. In certain circumstances, such as a large crowd anticipated for a small venue, methods of limiting or diverting the audience to ensure that this capacity is not exceeded may need to be investigated.

6.2 AUDIENCE PROFILE

The facilities will need to be different depending on the predominant age, sex and culture of the audience. For example attracting a family audience will necessitate additional provision for lost children and baby changing facilities; a large proportion of women in the audience may indicate a need for a higher proportion of female stewards and a different ratio of male/female toilets.

6.3 PROXIMITY OF THE AUDIENCE TO THE PERFORMERS

6.3.1 For a static show outdoor performers will often encourage the audience to be as close as possible. However the closer the audience the fewer number of people can see the show; by creating a bigger performance space more people can see the show. The delineation between the audience and the stage performance area can be created in a number of different ways depending on the risk

Sarruga, Liverpool Streets Ahead ©Liverpool City Council

Honey, Pif Paf Arts. SIRF ©Gilmar Ribeiro, gilmarribeiro.com

assessment of the show. For example a street theatre show may create this by simply laying a rope on the ground with stewards and/ or the performer talking to the audience advising them not to step over the rope. To assist the audience to see it is helpful to have at least part of the audience sitting on the ground – again good communication from the stewards will assist this process.

6.3.2 Walkabout performances create different problems because it is in the nature of the performance that performers will interact with passers by. In this instance it is impossible to maintain a gap between the performer and the audience. Experienced performers usually know how to deal with problems on the street (e.g. loutish or over excitable behaviour) but it is useful to have at least one person from the organisation to walk with the performer. Brief this person not to get too close and spoil the audiences' enjoyment; however they do need to be close enough to step in and deal with any problems that may occur.

6.4 AUDIENCE CONTROL

The risk assessment should determine the most appropriate means of controlling the audience whether this is by human resources (police, stewards) or barriers. There are some shows where provision of barriers can be counter-productive in terms of public safety. Therefore the location and type of barrier requires careful consideration.

07 MAKING EVENTS ACCESSIBLE

The terms of the Disability Discrimination Act (2005) makes it unlawful for service providers to discriminate against a disabled person for a reason related to their disability. The Act gives disabled people rights in the areas of:

1 Employment
2 Provision or acquisition of goods and services
3 Buying or renting land or property

Event organisers should budget to include access as part of their total festival budget from the beginning, rather than just seeing access as a separate facility to be added at a later stage. An Access Toolkit has been created by Independent Street Arts Network (ISAN) and Attitude is Everything. It is available as a free download from the ISAN website. It recognises that some organisations in the Street Arts sector are working with limited budgets and resources, and there is advice on using existing resources that companies may already have.

When considering how to make the event accessible organisers should consider a variety of impairments as not all disabled people are wheelchair users. Other impairments to be considered are:

→ People with mobility impairments
→ People with visual impairments
→ Deaf people and people who are hard of hearing
→ People with learning disabilities
→ People with mental health issues
→ People with hidden impairments

All aspects of provision for Deaf and disabled people should be considered from ensuring that the event and its access provision, is marketed in an accessible way, to providing training to staff to ensure that they are aware of the specific location of accessible facilities. For example, stewards need to know where to direct, disabled people to in order to utilise access provision, (such as a viewing platform or Sign Language interpreter), or this service may go unused. It is also important to consult with Deaf and disabled people in the planning process of the event in order to ensure that the access provision is adequate.

The ISAN Access Toolkit: Making outdoor arts events accessible to all, is available to download from www.streetartsnetwork.org.uk

Against the Tide. Graeae Theatre Company and Strange Fruit. G+DIF 2009. Alison Baskerville

08 PERFORMER REQUIREMENTS

The Angels, Larkin About. Paradise Gardens Festival 2008. Hayley Madden

8.1 PERFORMER LIAISON

Prior to the event there needs to be effective liaison with the performers. Often performers will provide a technical specification for the show such as the conditions that they need to perform the show, number of microphones, lighting requirements, crew and personnel required etc. However even for the simplest of shows it is essential to establish a dialogue with the performers about the safety considerations. Ideally each company should provide a risk assessment of their show; if they do not have a risk assessment the following checklist can be used as a starting point for a discussion with performers:

→ Site plan with all relevant items clearly marked e.g. light towers, pyrotechnic sites, sound position, Front of House position performer routes in and out of the space

→ Minimum stage area, audience area, backstage area

→ Surface requirements e.g. can the show be performed on grass, hard-standing, cobbles

→ A brief technical description of the show including any significant timings e.g. use of fireworks, entrances and exits etc. Details of fireworks, pyrotechnics or fire/flame effects including storage, transport and disposal details

→ Details of lighting (including any strobe lighting)

→ Structural calculations for any structures (over 2m high)

→ Details of electrically powered equipment or tools

→ Details of any lifting equipment

→ Details of debris left after the show and any special requirements for disposal of this material

→ Radio controlled equipment

Clearly this list can be considerably shorter for smaller performances.

The important point to note is to keep asking questions until satisfactory answers are received. With non-English speaking companies it is vital that information is translated accurately.

8.2 SPECIAL EFFECTS
One of the most exciting aspects of outdoor events is the spectacular elements of the show e.g. fire, water or pyrotechnic effects. It is important to stress that almost all of these activities can be managed safely providing that adequate time and resources are allocated. For all effects it is important to advise the public that there will be special effects. In particular you should advise the public about strobe effects, by giving both written and verbal warnings, as they can trigger epileptic fits.

8.2.1 FIRE This can include fire eating, fire juggling, naked flames in containers e.g. lanterns, fire pots. For naked flames the important consideration is to ensure that the audience is a safe distance away from the flame (this should take account of the wind conditions) and that there is suitable fire fighting equipment located near to the performance area. Fire-eaters often use paraffin to create the effect. Care should be taken that this is stored in suitable containers and that fire-eaters are aware of the potential for spills and the potentially harmful effects of spray caused by fire breathing.

Fire risk assessments should be completed in relation to the special risks associated with fire.

8.2.2 WATER EFFECTS Water and electricity do not mix well! Ensure that all water effects are located in a safe area away from electrics and consider the impact that wind may have on water sprays. All electrics should be earthed and supplied with waterproofed, outdoor cabling and have a Residual Current Detector (RCD). Organisers should be mindful of the Electricity at Work Regulations 1989 which requires electrical equipment to be maintained by a competent person, and should refer to the HSE leaflet Electrical Safety for Entertainers.

8.2.3 PYROTECHNIC EFFECTS Although all pyrotechnics are subject to European Union regulations there is sometimes a more "laissez faire" attitude to pyrotechnic effects in other European countries than in the UK. For example what is deemed to be acceptable in a Spanish Festival almost certainly will not be acceptable in the UK! It is important to work with the company to ensure that the integrity of the performance is not affected and that the safety of the public is not compromised. In some situations it may be advisable to employ a UK pyrotechnic specialist to work with the international company.

8.3 TEMPORARY STRUCTURES PROPS AND COSTUMES
These are an intrinsic part of many outdoor performances and are often constructed on a large scale to maximise the impact. Examples of temporary structures used include trapeze rigs, stage sets, and sculptures. For temporary structures located on the street that are over 2.4m there will be a requirement to produce structural calculations to assess the strength, durability, impact of wind etc. Full details can be found in the Institute of Structural Engineers' document *Temporary Demountable Structures: Guidance on design, procurement and use.* For structures such as marquees, stages or scaffolding these calculations should be readily available; however "home-made" structures may need to have calculations produced by a competent engineer. Check with the Local Authority's Building Control Officer if you are unsure. All set and props must be "weather resistant" and made from flame retardant materials. For all structures a signed completion certificate should be obtained from the contractor to confirm that it has been erected in accordance with the information provided earlier.

Institute of Structural Engineers' publications from: www.istructe.org

8.4 SITE SPECIFIC EVENTS
Some companies will adapt their performance to suit a particular location. For this type of show it is essential that there is a site visit well before the event to determine the most appropriate method of staging the event.

8.5 ON SITE FACILITIES
To ensure that the event goes smoothly consideration should be given to providing the following facilities near the performance area:
→ Secure parking for performers vehicles
→ Dressing rooms of sufficient size to accommodate the group(s) with tables, chairs, mirrors & drinking water
→ Performer only toilets (with separate facilities for children, and accessible toilets if required)
→ Route to and from the performance area
→ Stage management personnel
→ Artist liaison personnel

8.6 CHILDREN

For all performances involving children care should be taken to ensure that there are adequate facilities (such as separate boys and girls changing and toilet facilities) and adequate chaperoning by CRB checked people.

The Children (Performance) Regulations 1968 regulate children taking part in:
→ Theatre – where a charge is made
→ Modelling & Sport – where the child or any other person is paid (this is not an admission charge but a 'wage')
→ Activities in Licensed premises

Local authorities run a licensing system designed to protect the child and give prime consideration to their health, welfare and education. The regulations apply to all children from birth until they reach compulsory school leaving age.
A child may perform without a license for up to four days, but only if:
→ it is unpaid
→ no absence from school is required
→ no performances in the previous six months

Performances arranged by school, scouts, guides, youth clubs and similiar do not need a licence. The licensing authority is normally the local authority where the child lives. The person responsible for organising the production or event should apply for the licence

Applications should be submitted 21 days before the performance takes place. While licensed to perform the child must be in the care of a chaperone. This may be a local authority approved chaperone, the child's parent or an appointed tutor.

Each local authority (which in this case would be the London borough, county or unitary council – not the local district council) has its own procedures so it is essential to check with them in advance.

Mirage, Compagnie Oposito. G+DIF 2007 Alastair Muir

Carnivals and processions create a wonderful spectacle in the streets but they require a considerable amount of planning.

9.1 PARADE DIRECTOR

The management and communication are crucial aspects of the parade. One person should be appointed as Parade Director to control the whole event. This person should be responsible for assimilating all the information and communicating this to both the participants and the external authorities e.g. the police.

The Parade Director should prepare a briefing sheet for all the participants to ensure that they know:
→ The order of the parade
→ Key personnel
→ Health and safety information
→ The arrival point and time
→ The finish point and approximate time
→ Facilities provided

This briefing should also be given to the police and the highways authority.

9.2 CONTENT

There are 3 types of processions:

9.2.1 VEHICULAR This may consist of either decorated floats with performers and/or sound systems or purpose built processional vehicles with special effects. The safety of the construction needs to be considered in detail and the following is a checklist of items that need to be considered when constructing the float:
→ All decoration and items to be securely fixed

- → Dimensions of the structure must not exceed the lowest height or the narrowest width restriction on the route
- → No sharp objects should protrude from the sides
- → Materials and fabrics should have the relevant fire certification
- → Any generators should be securely fastened, earthed, RCD protected
- → Suitable fire extinguishers need to be located on each float
- → Safety handrails should be around any exposed sides
- → Sufficient protection around the wheels

For existing vehicles as part of a show there should be drawings and information about the vehicle. In both cases a maximum speed limit should be imposed.

9.2.2 PEDESTRIAN PROCESSIONS The important factors to consider when planning the route are:
- → The composition of the participants – does it include disabled people, children, stilt walkers
- → The type of costumes or set
- → The profile of the proposed route e.g. if it is uphill the procession should be shorter.

9.2.3 COMBINATION Both vehicles and pedestrians in the procession. This may include bicycles, handcarts or motorised vehicles. The key aspect of this parade is ensuring that the vehicles and pedestrians do not collide by imposing a walking pace speed limit and employing competent drivers.

9.2.4 FIREWORKS Many companies like to use flares, firecrackers and small pyrotechnic effects as part of the parade. It is important to have fire stewards with fire fighting equipment e.g. fire extinguishers and a number of metal buckets (with a small amount of sand) in which to put spent flares.

9.3 THE ROUTE

9.3.1 LIAISON Prior to creating a procession it is essential that the police, ambulance, fire brigade, bus/taxis and the local authority be consulted. A parade is essentially a very large slow moving vehicle and it is essential that all parties are aware of the detail of the parade.

It may be necessary to formally close roads to traffic for the duration of the event. This must be done through the Council's Highways Department (which may be separate from a district or

Liverpool Lord Mayors Parade 2008. Liverpool Capital of Culture, ©Liverpool Culture Company

borough council). Road Traffic Orders normally require at least 3 months to be arranged.

Most police forces are now insisting that a formal road closure be in place in order that they can enforce a road closure. Whilst the police do have the power to close a road for an emergency increasingly their view is that, as this is a planned activity, a road closure order is required. This can be obtained by contacting the

Local Authority Traffic Department. There may be cost associated with advertising the route and the administration of the Road Traffic Order. It is advisable that a police vehicle be at the rear of the parade to ensure that other vehicles do not attempt to "overtake" the parade and also that consideration is given to all the side roads that enter on to the proposed route. When planning a circular route be careful that a large area of the town or city is not completely encircled preventing traffic flow in and out of the area.

9.3.2 TIMING For any event it is important to minimise the length of time a road closure is in effect in order to minimise the inconvenience to other road users. The time of day is also an important feature e.g. it is unlikely that a road closure will be permitted at 5 pm on a busy commuter route. It is also imperative that the procession starts and finishes within the time allowed and that there is a cautious estimate of the total time taken from the moment of leaving the assembly area to the whole parade arriving at the finale area. It is easier to reopen roads faster than planned rather than keeping them closed for longer than planned.

9.3.3. ASSEMBLY AREA The assembly of a parade can be a very long process. For this reason it is worth considering assembling the parade off the road e.g. in a car park or park. Ensure that there is sufficient space for car parking and for the parade to line up in the correct order (this may be in a zig zag formation). Parade marshals are essential to ensure that the groups line up correctly.

9.3.4. ROUTE A careful assessment should be made of the whole route taking into account not just the immediate route but also the potential effect on subsidiary routes. Organisers should be aware of potential "pinch points" on the route where large vehicles or processional pieces may have difficulty turning or passing crowds or obstacles. Check the height and width of the largest object to ensure that it can pass through the route, taking account of obstructions for example street furniture including rubbish bins and lampposts. In the event of an emergency situation developing either within the parade (for example a vehicle breakdown) or outside the control of the parade (for example a fire in an adjacent building), a contingency route should be identified.

9.3.5 FACILITIES EN ROUTE Consideration should be given to facilities for the participants en route. It is essential that first aid travel behind the parade and that in a long parade there are drinks (particularly water) for the participants.

9.3.6 FINALE AREA Like the assembly area this should be large enough to accommodate the whole parade and it is preferable that this is off the road. If this is in a different location to the assembly point consideration may need to be given to transporting the participants back to the starting point. Refreshments and shelter for the participants should also be considered.

9.4 CROWD CONTROL

9.4.1 THE ROUTE Consideration should be given to ensuring that the crowd do not obstruct the parade route. An arrowhead formation of stewards and/or police can be used to part the crowd to enable the parade to pass through safely. At specific pinch points barriers and stewards may be required to ensure that the audience are kept a suitable distance from the parade.

9.4.2 MOVING PARADES INTO A STATIC CROWD One of the key problems is a moving parade entering an event location where a crowd has already assembled. Crowds will inevitably try to get as close as possible to the action so it is important that if a parade is moving into an area that is already occupied that there is sufficient expansion room to enable people to move out of the way. Alternatively it may be necessary to create a clear area for the parade and any following crowd to enter (see appendix 2 Case Study 1 for a practical example).

9.4.3 STEWARDS AND POLICE As mentioned earlier, the police will have been involved in the planning of any parade. However this does not necessarily mean that they will steward the event.

Although the police should be involved in the planning of the parade it is not their responsibility to steward the parade; it is their responsibility to maintain public order.

Ensure that you have sufficient stewards to assist the parade to keep moving. Extensive briefing of police and stewards, preferably with a 'walk through' prior to the event is essential to ensure that the event goes smoothly. Ideally, for a large-scale parade the front should be in radio contact with the rear of the event. If the parade is noisy radio headsets will be required to ensure that communication is maintained.

10 CONCLUSION

Les Rous de Couleurs (Compagnie Off) G+DIF 2006. Doug Southall, Pepper Pictures

Street Arts events by their very nature do not fit into a specific formula and therefore it is imperative that the organiser of an event of this type undertakes a risk assessment which is specific to the particular circumstances created by the performance and location. With sufficient planning and forethought, almost any hazardous activity can be made safe with the use of adequate control measures.

The development of a safety plan for an event of this nature will be a creative and fluid process which will need to be amended to take account of changing circumstances. By keeping all interested parties involved in the process your event should take place within a safe environment.

New Year's Eve. Newcastle 2001. Theatre Titanik N. D. S. Produced by Event International. Newcastle City Council

This risk assessment has been prepared by Event International Ltd based on previous New Years Eve events in 1998 and 1999 and updated after discussion with the Safety Advisory Group.

In compiling these assessments due regard has been taken of the recommendations of the Health and Safety Executive guidance contained within The Event Safety Guide: A guide to health, safety and welfare at music and similar events and Managing Crowds Safely.

Event International Ltd has appointed a Safety Co-ordinator, David Bilton, who has achieved the National Examination Board of Occupational Safety and Health (NEBOSH) General Certificate and has been instrumental in writing these risk assessments in conjunction with the Production Manager. The Safety Co-ordinator will be in attendance from the beginning of the event to the end of the event and will have no conflicting roles during this period.

One of the major determining factors in the risk assessment has been the anticipated crowd numbers. The Parade crowd is anticipated to be less than 12,000 and therefore the decision has been taken not to limit the numbers and allow free, uninhibited access.

One of the key factors in minimising the risks associated with this sort of event is the experience and number of stewards at the event. The steward company was appointed after a tender process with references taken from six other events, which were all satisfactory. They have been a part of the planning process and attended Safety Advisory Group meetings and operational meetings as appropriate.

Event Control is the key link between the Chief Steward, Event Organisers and the Police located at The Civic Centre, Haymarket.

In order to assess risks, the following indices have been used:

PROBABLE FREQUENCY
1 = Improbable
2 = Unlikely
3 = Possible / happens
4 = Happens occasionally
5 = Happens periodically
6 = Happens frequently

SEVERITY
1 = Trivial
2 = Minor
3 = Major – single
4 = Major – multiple
5 = Hospitalisation
6 = Fatality

RISK ASSESSMENT: RIG AND DERIG

HAZARD	RISK	POTENTIAL NUMBERS	FREQUENCY (A)	SEVERITY (B)	RATING (A×B)	CONTROL MEASURES	REVISED FREQUENCY (A)	REVISED SEVERITY (B)	REVISED RATING (A×B)
Plant and machinery	Injuring public	<20	3	3	9	→ Working compounds to be created with 2m barriers → If there is no working compound Steward/s to supervise public where required	1	3	3
Vehicles unloading equipment	Bus stops blocked Danger to public	<20	3	3	9	→ Bus stops to be moved from Barras Bridge 28 December – 2 January → Passage of equipment from vehicle to site to be stewarded where appropriate	1	3	3
Fireworks	Display to be lit inadvertently	25	2	4	8	→ Safe compounds to be created at all fireworks rigging sites with strict no smoking rules in the vicinity	1	4	4
Equipment drops	Equipment dropped in wrong place causing danger to public and need to move it whilst public are there	25	2	2	4	→ All contractors to be sent detailed instructions as to dates, times and exact place of drop off. → Site managers to be in place to meet drops	1	2	2

RISK ASSESSMENT: THE PARADE

HAZARD	RISK	POTENTIAL NUMBERS	FREQUENCY (A)	SEVERITY (B)	RATING (A×B)	CONTROL MEASURES	REVISED FREQUENCY (A)	REVISED SEVERITY (B)	REVISED RATING (A×B)
Haymarket, Parade entering crowded area	Public being crushed	2000	4	4	16	→ Crowd and parade to be kept in separate areas at Monument and Haymarket and entrance to Northumberland Street to enable the following crowd to filter into a sterile area. (See parade diagrams)	2	4	8
Northumberland Street overcrowding:	Public being crushed	1000	3	4	12	→ Parade to be stewarded at the front, back and sides. Consideration was given to creating a sterile area for the parade with barriers/tape. However this idea rejected, as it will create problems due to confining the crowd within an already confined space. Vehicles will be instructed to drive very slowly and stewards will clear the space in front. If necessary the crowd can be "pushed" into the sterile area at the top of Northumberland Street (plan)	2	3	6
Commencement of parade	Fireworks setting off main display	30	2	3	6	→ No aerial display permitted	1	2	2
Slope up Grey Street	Vehicles slipping back	1000	3	4	12	→ Route to be gritted dependent on weather → Volunteers recruited to pull vehicles up the slope if required All vehicles to have adequate brake facilities	1	4	4
Parade vehicle access	Hitting obstructions	100	3	4	12	→ The parade will follow the designated "roadway" up Northumberland Street which has adequate height clearance → Xmas light catenaries to be taken down prior to 31·12·00 → Walk through on the 30·12·00 to be attended by Event Production Manager, Police rep, Safety Co-ordinator and steward rep. to ensure route is clear	1	4	4
Firebrands carried by volunteers	Injuries to public/ performers	20	3	3	9	→ 4 weekends training by company → No persons under 16 to be allowed in the Parade	2	3	6
Crowds	Public disorder	100	3	4	12	→ Stewards to be fully briefed verbally and in writing → Police in attendance throughout	2	3	6
Fireworks	Finale fireworks					→ See separate risk assessment from fireworks contractor			
Scaffolding	Climbing and falling	10	3	3	9	→ All scaffold to be assessed one month before the parade and letter sent to company	2	3	6
Traffic	Traffic and public mingling	250	4	5	20	→ Extensive road closures as detailed in section x to ensure event area is traffic free → Swan House roundabout to be closed by police until parade has passed	1	4	4
Street furniture	Trips and obstruction	100	4	3	12	→ Street furniture as per attached plan will be removed	1	3	3

APPENDIX 02: CASE STUDIES 01: PROCESSION

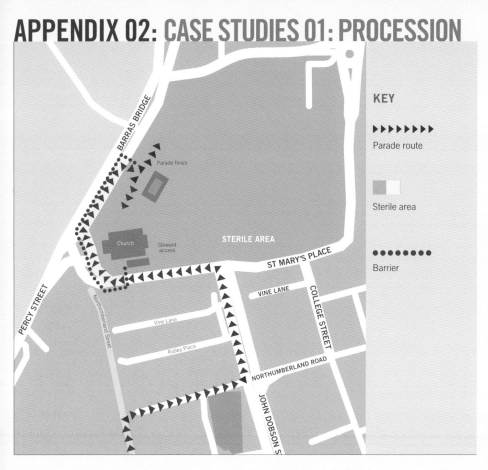

KEY

▶▶▶▶▶▶▶▶
Parade route

Sterile area

●●●●●●●●
Barrier

Parade finish

Church

Steward access

STERILE AREA

BARRAS BRIDGE

PERCY STREET

Northumberland Street

Vine Lane

Ridley Place

ST MARY'S PLACE

VINE LANE

COLLEGE STREET

NORTHUMBERLAND ROAD

JOHN DOBSON S

'push' through a dense crowd. This was done by creating a barriered access route to the finale site, thus keeping the route clear. Entrance to this access point was controlled by a steward cordon which opened to allow the procession into the finale area at the appropriate time. Location of the access point was determined following a request from the Church who wanted to retain access to enable refreshments to be served; this was able to be accommodated after discussions with the Local Authority and Police.

The steward cordon prevented access until the procession arrived; they then closed the cordon again after the parade had entered to enable the vehicles to manoeuvre. There was a contingency to open this cordon again if the crowd density was becoming a problem as it created some expansion room. However this could only be made by the Joint Event Control where representatives from the event organisers, police, and Steward Company were located.

EVENT
Newcastle New Year's Eve Celebrations. This is a processional event which starts in the centre of the city and finishes with a pyrotechnic finale – also in the City Centre.

THE PROBLEM
The event has been running successfully for a number of years and whilst a crowd gathers at the start of the parade there is now also a large crowd (circa 10,000) which gathers at the finale site waiting for the procession to arrive and the fireworks finale. This has meant that a vehicular procession followed by a large pedestrian crowd was trying to

access the finale site through a packed crowd. Whilst normally a procession can move through a crowd safely with good stewarding (and police support where necessary) this situation was different in that there was a dense crowd without the ability to move into additional space. The procession was approximately 100m long and 3m wide – so potentially up to 600 people had to be moved to enable the parade to pass through.

THE SOLUTION
The solution was to create a method of ensuring that the procession did not have to

POINTS TO NOTE
Stewards, police, first aiders and other officials need to ensure that they don't follow the parade in to the finale area and block viewing with a sea of fluorescent jackets.

This operation depends on good communication between event officials, stewards and Police. The joint event control situated in a remote position with radio and phone communications was vital to ensure that information could be relayed from the finale area to the procession and vice versa.

Early morning: a rocket is discovered in Waterloo Place, London. The Sultan's Elephant Royal de Luxe, Produced by Artichoke, May 2006 Photo © Sophie Laslett courtesy Arts Council England

May 2006. The Sultan's Elephant – a four day piece of street theatre by French company Royal de Luxe, proposed to take place in central London. An exotic Sultan in a far-away land commissions a time-travelling machine from his favourite professor. The machine arrives in the form of a 12m high, 40 tonne mechanical elephant. A small girl (a giant 8m high) in an early 20th Century space rocket crash lands in the city and makes the acquaintance of the Sultan and his magical companions.

THE PROBLEM

How to persuade the authorities and potential funders that this magical idea was something that could be made real. The proposed disruption was considerable, and while central London closes itself down on a regular basis for events of national significance, ranging from the London Marathon to the Trooping of the Colour, it was unprecedented for these crucial ceremonial routes to give themselves up for a piece of fantastical story-telling.

THE SOLUTION

Fortunately, the piece was to be premiered in the company's home town of Nantes in France in the summer of 2005. The main operational partners from Westminster City Council, the Metropolitan Police and Transport for London were invited to Nantes to see how the show worked. The leaders of these agencies and authorities bought into the project on the premise that they had seen it successfully performed in a large French provincial town. The show worked, but everyone knew there would be some hefty logistical issues. London is a major capital city with millions of occupants and a complex transport infrastructure.

The psychological advantage was now with the event. Anyone throwing up their hands in horror would upset somebody higher up in their organisations, so the momentum of peer pressure took over.

WATERLOO PLACE: INSTALLATION

The first day involves the crash-landing of the Little Girl's space rocket in Waterloo Place between the Institute of Directors and The Carlton Club. Royal de Luxe were insistent that, in order to create the illusion of a real crash, a large part of the parking area should be dug up to allow the insertion of a steel frame 2m below the surface that could carry the weight of the rocket. The rocket was craned into place, bolted onto the frame, a smoke machine inserted beneath and the tarmac reapplied and dressed to look as if it had been shattered on impact.

Dig a hole in a City and you have no idea what you are going to find unless you do a detailed survey involving water, drainage, gas, electricity, telephone lines laid by any number of companies and the dreaded fibreoptics and cable networks. Added to which Royal de Luxe, regarding the whole enterprise as part of the artistic conception of the show, were determined to do the digging themselves. Just this small part of the overall event promised to be an almighty challenge. Bit by bit, permission by permission over a period of three months, the barriers were eventually broken down. The key to success was the loyalty and determination to make the show a reality that had been built up with all the agencies and authorities. Eventually it was agreed that although UK contractors were to supervise the works, the digging was actually done by Royale de Luxe. Although in many ways, the project was dominated by a lack of orthodoxy, everyone involved discovered a new and more flexible approach to problem-solving. It was discovered that problems usually only exist in the minds of those who are trained to say 'no', rather than taking responsibility for saying 'yes'. It was successfully argued that London's roads are dug up every day of the week (maybe not for a fairytale); the end product – a hole – is the same if it's for an electrical cable, a watermain or a rocket. And it always gets filled in again.

It takes a Herculean effort to engage all of a city's many agencies – but in the end it was discovered that it's not the agencies as institutions that make the difference – but more the individuals within them who are prepared to think differently, to take a bit of a risk and to lead where perhaps their more nervous colleagues are less prepared to follow. Events such as these are difficult, but only because we imagine that it's somehow illegitimate to turn our cities into playgrounds. Perhaps if we did it more often, we wouldn't be so anxious…

11 APPENDIX 02 CASE STUDY 03: ACCESS AUDIT

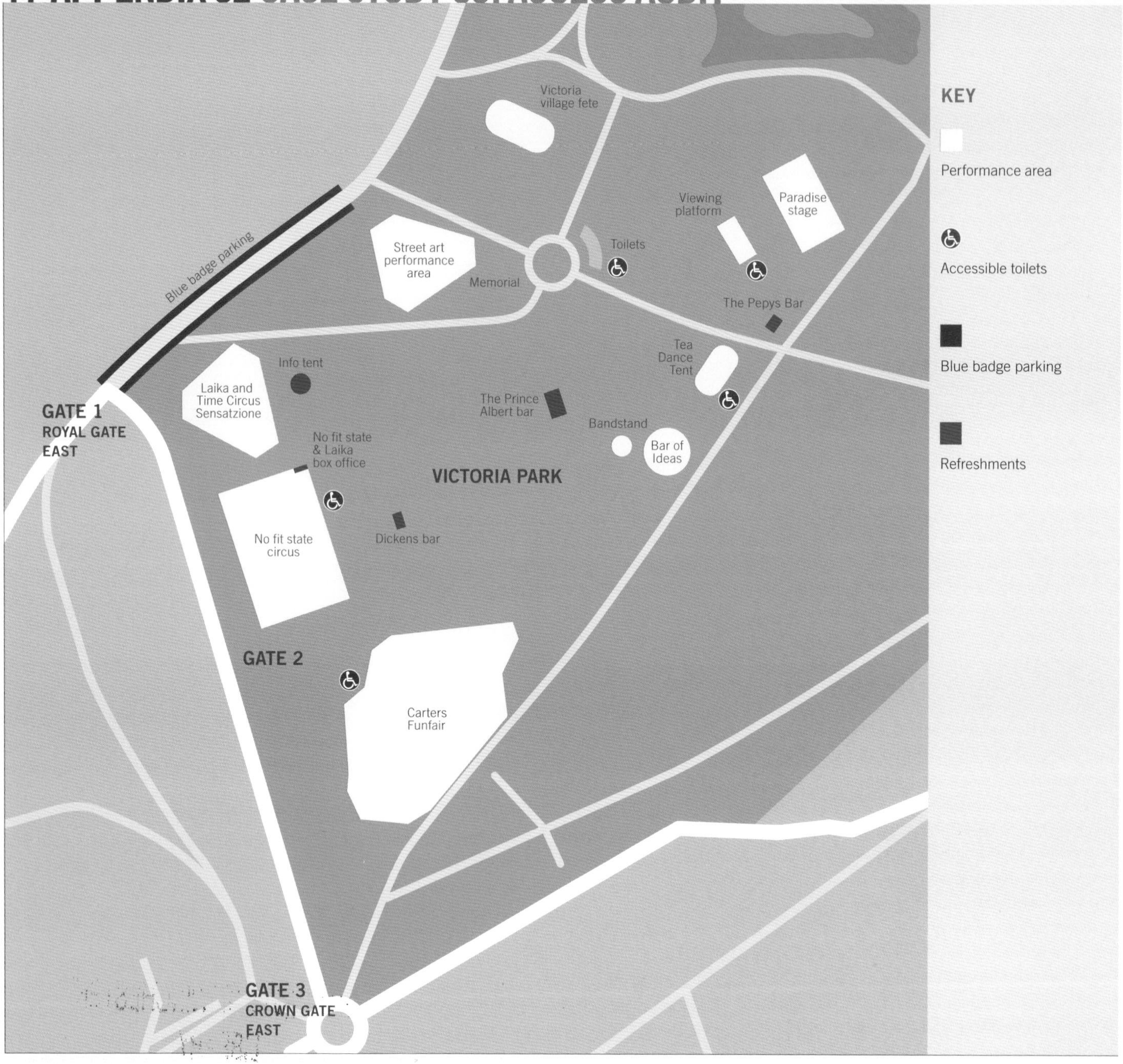

Victoria village fete
Street art performance area
Memorial
Toilets
Viewing platform
Paradise stage
The Pepys Bar
Tea Dance Tent
Blue badge parking
Info tent
Laika and Time Circus Sensatzione
GATE 1
ROYAL GATE EAST
The Prince Albert bar
Bandstand
Bar of Ideas
No fit state & Laika box office
VICTORIA PARK
No fit state circus
Dickens bar
GATE 2
Carters Funfair
GATE 3
CROWN GATE EAST
KEY
Performance area
Accessible toilets
Blue badge parking
Refreshments

EVENT ORGANISERS
Remarkable Productions Ltd for London Borough of Tower Hamlets

EVENT
Paradise Gardens Festival, Victoria Park east London

Paradise Gardens takes the idea of a Victorian pleasure garden and updates it for the 21st Century, offering a wide array of artforms, stages and activities for audiences of all ages to enjoy. The site is approximately 17 hectares and level with open areas, some mature trees and is relatively easy to move around via tarmac paths.

THE APPROACH
Attitude is Everything were brought in to undertake training (before and during the event), to undertake an access audit and to work with the organisers to produce an action plan with short, medium and long term objectives.

TRAINING
A Disability Equality Training day was held with key personnel. The training provided a brief background in the legal requirements of the Disability Discrimination Act (1995), and illustrated the Social Model of Disability, which defines disability as the effect upon the lives of people with impairments, through oppression, discrimination, inequality of opportunity and living in an inaccessible environment. In short, disability is the experience of barriers to participation.

Festival staff were encouraged to use the training, and their existing knowledge of the festival to identify areas where access could be improved and to draw up an action plan with clearly identifiable outcomes.

On the day of the event stewards were given a briefing by Attitude is Everything on the location of key facilities and routes, and how to assist Deaf and disabled audience members appropriately. The Chief Steward actively endorsed the training and ensured that it was followed by the stewards.

THE ACTIONS
PUBLICITY A downloadable, text-only version of the flyer, was produced which included access information e.g. public transport, parking, distances to and on site. A dedicated email address was made available for any access queries.

ON SITE As there were strict parking controls in the surrounding streets, parking provision for disabled people was created which was well located with paths running from it to the rest of the site.

→ Careful consideration was given to the siting of tents and stages in relation to paths, to minimise the amount of 'off road' needed to get to them.

→ A viewing platform was installed with excellent sight-lines to the main stage.

→ Accessible toilets were distributed to minimise the distance from any point on site.

→ Guy ropes, tent poles and pegs and other trip hazards were highlighted, and cable runs buried or covered.

→ Volunteers offered British Sign Language in the information tent.

THE FUTURE
The Attitude is Everything access audit report identified a number of further actions to be undertaken, and the production team themselves decided to work differently in a number of areas:

Access provision is to be built into event preparation from the earliest stages, and an access statement should appear on all publicity material.

Better promotion of access facilities is needed to ensure the public are aware of them, for example the viewing platform, which was under-used, and any BSL or Audio Description services

The installation of toilets, platforms, handrails, floor coverings and cable runs need to be checked and signed off from an access point of view before contractors leave site to enable issues to be rectified.

A review of the style and location of on site signage is required, and a greater variety of chairs needs to be made available at areas across the site.

More BSL provision and Audio Description of events is desirable.

All of these actions, together with a commitment to continually review the accessibility of the event, will lead to a better experience for both Deaf and disabled artists and audiences. In addition, the numbers of Deaf and disabled people attending the event will increase.

NOTES